Re

# A Little Book of Quips and Quotes

Compiled by Hugh Morrison

Montpelier Publishing

London 2015

ISBN-13: 978-1519206350
ISBN-10: 1519206356

Published by Montpelier Publishing, London

Cover image by Aleutie

'Why are you always reading that book on pensions?'

'I'm trying to work out how much money I'll save by not having one.'


Smith retired, and announced to his wife that he would spend his new-found spare time growing all the vegetables they required in the garden. 'In a few months' time we won't be wondering whether we can buy them on just a pension.' 'No,' replied his wife. 'We'll be wondering how they manage to sell them so cheaply in the shops.'


Former MP (to government minister): You promised me a job when I retired.'

Minister: But there are no jobs.

Former MP: I need a job.

Minister: Well, I'll set up a commission to investigate why there are no jobs and you can get a job on that.


Definition of luxuries: things that were necessities before you retired.

We have just learnt of a teacher who started with nothing twenty years ago and who has retired with the comfortable fortune of two hundred thousand pounds. This was acquired through industry, economy, conscientious effort, indomitable perseverance, and the death of an uncle who left her an estate valued at £199,999.50.

'What's your husband getting for his retirement?'

'Bald and fat.'

What does secret agent 007 become when he retires?

A Pensioner Bond.

**A retirement card greeting:**

Don't think about the past; your work here was well done.

Don't think about the future; there are many years to come.

Don't think about the present; we didn't get you one!

Doris from Personnel was a bit of a show off and when she retired, her colleagues asked her what she'd like for a present. 'Oh I don't know,' she simpered. 'Something with lots of diamonds?' So they bought her a pack of cards.

It was the birthday of Miss Smith, the glamorous secretary in the publicity department, and also the last day on the job for old Fred, the office caretaker.

The boss bought a bottle of perfume for Miss Smith, and wrote a note saying 'Use this on yourself and think of me.' He bought Fred a shotgun, and wrote a note saying 'Here's something for next time you go hunting. I hope you catch something interesting.'

The presents were duly delivered by the boss' secretary; the perfume to Miss Smith and the shotgun to Fred. Unfortunately she mixed the notes up.

Deirdre had worked for the company for so long that nobody could remember how many years she'd served. The boss was preparing his speech for the retirement party and asked her 'When did you start working here?' 'When you told me you'd sack me if I didn't,' replied Deirdre.

A retired husband is often a wife's full-time job. *Ella Harris*

There was an article in the company magazine about the importance of paying into the company pension scheme. The headline was 'I upped my contributions – up yours!'

The best time to start thinking about your retirement is before the boss does.

Coming up to 65, Jones began to worry that his pension arrangements were not sufficient, so he went to see a financial advisor.

'My fee will be £500 an hour,' said the advisor.

'I'm here to solve my financial problems, not yours,' said Jones.

Gladys was retiring, and her colleagues asked her what she'd like as a present. 'Oh I don't know,' she said vaguely. 'Just a little something to remind me of the happy times I spent here.' So they presented her with a tea kettle and a lavatory seat.

## The perks of being over 60:

1) Kidnappers are not very interested in you.
2) In a hostage situation you are likely to be released first.
3) No one expects you to run -- anywhere.
4) People call at 9 PM and ask, 'Did I wake you?'
5) People no longer view you as a hypochondriac.
6) There is nothing left to learn the hard way.
7) Things you buy now won't wear out.
8) You can eat dinner at 4 p.m.
9) You can live without sex but not without your glasses.
10) You enjoy hearing about other peoples' operations.
11) You get into heated arguments about pension plans.
12) You no longer think of speed limits as a challenge.
13) You quit trying to hold your stomach in, no matter who walks into the room.
14) You sing along with elevator music.
15) Your eyes won't get much worse.
16) Your investment in health insurance is finally beginning to pay off.
17) Your joints are more accurate meteorologists than the national weather service.

18) Your secrets are safe with your friends because they can't remember them either.

19) Your supply of brain cells is finally down to manageable size.

20) You can't remember the book where you saw this list.

There is an enormous number of managers who have retired on the job. *Peter F. Drucker*

Today we would like to thank Nigel for his service to our company. Nigel is someone who does not know the meaning of impossible task, who does not know the meaning of lunch break, who does not understand the meaning of the word no. So we have clubbed together and bought him a dictionary.

When an English teacher in Italy retired, he received a card from one of his pupils which read 'I thank you from the heart of my bottom.'

The trouble with retirement is that you never get a day off. *Abe Lemons*

When a man retires, his wife gets twice the husband but only half the income. *Chi Chi Rodriguez*

**What those retirement speeches really mean...**

1. *Active socially*: Drinks heavily.
2. *Character above reproach*: Still one step ahead of the law.
3. *Excells in the effective application of skills*: Makes a good cup of coffee.
4. *Internationally known*: Likes to go to conferences and trade shows in Europe.
5. *Is well informed*: Knows all office gossip and where all the skeletons are kept.
6. *Tactful in dealing with superiors*: Knows when to keep mouth shut.
7. *Willing to take calculated risks*: Doesn't mind spending someone else's money.

Retired is being twice tired, I've thought
First tired of working, then tired of not.
*Richard Armour*

I've been attending lots of seminars in my retirement. They're called naps. *Merri Brownworth*

I'm retired — goodbye tension, hello pension!

Retirement: the world's longest coffee break.

If people concentrated on the really important things in life, there'd be a shortage of fishing poles. *Doug Larson*

Retirement is wonderful. It's doing nothing without worrying about getting caught at it. *Gene Perret*

There are some who start their retirement long before they stop working. *Robert Half*

When you retire, think and act as if you were still working; when you're still working, think and act a bit as if you were already retired.

The question isn't at what age I want to retire, it's at what income. *George Foreman*

Retirement means no pressure, no stress, no heartache... unless you play golf. *Gene Perret*

Golf is played by twenty million mature American men whose wives think they are out having fun. *Jim Bishop*

Don't play too much golf. Two rounds a day are plenty. *Harry Vardon*

Youth would be an ideal state if it came a little later in life. *Herbert Asquith*

Half our life is spent trying to find something to do with the time we have rushed through life trying to save. *Will Rogers*

When you retire, you switch bosses — from the one who hired you to the one who married you. *Gene Perret*

I'm now as free as the breeze — with roughly the same income. *Gene Perret*

When a man retires and time is no longer a matter of urgent importance, his colleagues generally present him with a watch. *R.C. Sherriff*

A gold watch is the most appropriate gift for retirement, as its recipients have given up so many of their golden hours in a lifetime of service. *Harry Mahtar*

Retirement is like a long vacation in Vegas. The goal is to enjoy these years to the fullest, but not so fully that you run out of money. *Jonathan Clements*

You are only young once, but you can stay immature indefinitely. *Ogden Nash*

In my retirement I go for a short swim at least once or twice every day. It's either that or buy a new golf ball. *Gene Perret*

The money's no better in retirement but the hours are! *Terri Guillemets*

'If my boss doesn't take back what he said, I'm going to have to start thinking about retirement.'

'What did he say?'

'"You should start thinking about retirement"'

Retirement: That's when you return from work one day and say, 'Hi, Honey, I'm home — forever.' *Gene Perret*

As you get older, you start thinking more about the hereafter. Every time I go into a room I find myself thinking, 'What am I here after?'

Retirement can be a great joy if you can work out how to spend time without spending money.

A Catholic priest was being honoured at his retirement dinner after 25 years in the parish. A leading local politician, who was also a member of the congregation, was chosen to make the presentation and give a speech at the dinner. He was delayed so the priest decided to say his own few words while they waited.

'I got my first impression of the parish from the first confession I heard here. I thought I had been assigned to a terrible place. The very first person who entered my confessional told me he had stolen a car and, when stopped by the police, had almost murdered the officer. He had stolen money from his parents, embezzled from his place of business, had an affair with his boss's wife, taken drugs. I was appalled. But as the days went on I knew that my people were not all like that and I had, indeed, come to a fine parish full of good and loving people.'

Just as the priest finished his talk the politician arrived full of apologies at being late. He immediately began to make the presentation and give his speech.

'I'll never forget the first day our parish priest arrived,' said the politician. 'In fact, I had the honour of being the first one to go to him in confession.'

My wife said, 'What are you doing today?'

I said, 'Nothing.'

She said, 'You did that yesterday.'

I said, 'I haven't finished yet.'

Two old men were discussing their working lives. The first said 'I remember my boss threw a great retirement party for me, thanked me for all my work and wished me all the best.' 'Sounds great,' said his friend. 'Not really,' said the first man. 'I was 35 at the time.'

When is a retiree's bedtime? Three hours after he falls asleep on the sofa.

**Retirement is having nothing to do and someone always keeping you from it.** *Robert Brault*

'I see Dr Brown in Proctology has finally retired.'

'Yes – he'd had the end in sight for some time.'

'Smith from Accounts says he's going to get a job as a dustbin man when he retires.'

'Why's that?'

'He thinks they only work on Wednesdays.'

How many retirees does it take to change a light bulb? Only one, but it might take all day.

Q. Why does a retiree often say he doesn't miss work, but misses the people he used to work with?

A. He is too polite to tell the whole truth.

## Music suggestions for a retirement party

*You're So Varicose Vein* by Carly Simon
*How Can You Mend A Broken Hip?* by the Bee Gees
*The First Time Ever I Forgot Your Face* by Roberta Flack
*I Can't See Clearly Now* by Johnny Nash
*These Boots Give Me Arthritis* by Nancy Sinatra
*You Make Me Feel Like Napping* by Leo Sayer
*I Want Your Specs* by George Michael
*A Whiter Shade of Hair* by Procol Harum
*Talking 'Bout My Medication* by the Who
*Zimmer Lovin'* by John Travolta and Olivia Newton-John
*Bald Thing* by the Troggs

A retired gentleman, finding himself rather bored, went for a job interview at his local supermarket. The interviewer looked at him doubtfully. 'Are you sure this will be suitable for you? You'll only be working two days a week, from ten a.m. to four p.m. You'll have to answer to a superior who's much younger than you, and you'll only be getting the minimum wage. 'Sounds great,' said the man. 'In fact that's exactly what I did for the last 30 years in full time work.'

What is so special about the age sixty-five? It is the time when one acquires sufficient experience to lose one's job through forced retirement.

The government recently noticed that it had too many colonels in the army and offered an early retirement package plus a £10,000 bonus for every inch measured in a straight line along the retiring officer's body between any two points he chose.

The first colonel accepted. He asked the pension man to measure from the top of his head to the tip of his toes. 6 feet. He walked out with a check for £720,000.

The second colonel asked them to measure from the tip of his outstretched hands to his toes. 8 feet. He walked away £960,000. When the third officer was asked where to measure, he told the pension man, 'from my index finger of the left foot to the thumb.' The pension man said 'My God!' he said, 'where is your thumb?!' The colonel replied, 'Iraq.'

'Never mind the company pension scheme – I'm just hoping I can pay off my student loan before I retire.'

'Why are you retiring at 55?' asked the boss to an employee. 'You have a secure job.' 'Only because nobody else wants it,' replied the worker.

I enjoy waking up and not having to go to work. So I do it three or four times a day. *Gene Perret*

A woman was explaining to her friend how her husband started walking a mile each day when he retired at 65. Each year he had added another mile – so two miles a day when he turned 66 and three miles a day when he was 67, and so on. 'He's 80 now,' said the woman. 'That sounds great,' said her friend. 'He must be very fit.' 'Maybe,' said the woman, 'the only trouble is I don't know where he is.'

Retirement: It's nice to get out of the rat race, but you have to learn to get along with less cheese. *Gene Perret*

Sid was retiring after 20 years working as a lavatory cleaner at King's Cross station in London. 'The first ten years were tough,' he recalled in his retirement speech, 'but after that, they gave me a brush.'

Q. What do you call Postman Pat when retires?

A. Pat.

After many years of contributing a portion of my salary to the company pension scheme, I decided to retire once I'd got to 65. Then I realised it probably wasn't a good idea to give up work on a pension pot of sixty-five pounds.

Regular naps prevent old age, especially if you take them while driving.

You know it's time to retire when your back goes out more than you do.

A man is known by the company that keeps him on after retirement age.

A man retired and went to sort out his pension at the social security office. When he got there, the receptionist asked for proof of his age. He realised he'd forgotten it. The receptionist thought for a moment, then said, 'open your shirt.' The man unbuttoned his shirt to reveal a large amount of curly white chest hair. 'That's good enough for me,' said the receptionist, and approved his application. When he got home he told his wife what had happened. 'It's a pity you didn't open your trousers as well,' said his wife. 'Then you might have qualified for disability too.'

A Chief Executive finally retired, and gave his wife the following strict instructions: 'Every morning you will wake me at 6.00 am and say "time to get up for the office, dear". And I will turn over, say "damn the office" and go back to sleep.'

Jones (to boss): I'm 65 next month and my wife is keen for me to retire. She wants me to redecorate the entire house, remodel the garden and for us to spend the weekends at the shopping centre.

Boss: I can't possibly let you retire, Jones. You're far too valuable to the firm.

Jones: Thank you sir – that's wonderful news!


Youth would be an ideal state if it came a little later in life. *Herbert Asquith*


A singer decided to retire and, wanting to go out on a high note, recorded a very overblown, emotional song in a voice that was clearly past its best. 'Did you hear my last record?' he asked a friend. 'I hope so,' came the reply.


A policeman was retiring and his inspector gave him a choice of two presents: £1000 in cash or a long service engraved gold medal. 'How much is the medal worth?' asked the constable. 'I suppose an intrinsic value of about one hundred pounds,' replied the inspector. 'In that case,' said the constable, 'I'll take the medal and £900.'


New Bank Director: What do you mean, retirement cured your deafness?'

Former Director: As soon as the amount of my pension got mentioned in the paper, I heard from my ex-wife.


'I see that famous graffiti artist has retired.'

'Yes, the writing had been on the wall for some time.'


It was the sixty-fifth birthday of the Human Resources Director and he announced to the boss, 'I've decided not to retire. I'll stay here for as long as the company needs me.' The boss thought for a moment and said 'Will you have a cup of tea before you go?'


A retirement toast: 'Here's champagne to your real friends, and real pain to your sham friends.'


'I'm interested in the low-cost pension contributions scheme.'

'Certainly sir. That will be £4.99 per month.'

'I'll take it.'

'Would sir like any extras with it?'

'Such as what?'

'Such as a pension?'

'When I retired I decided to start jogging every morning. The doctor told me it would add years to my life. He was right – I've only been retired a week and I feel ten years older already.'


Smith retired but however hard he tried he couldn't cure himself of the habit of waking up at 6.00 am with a start, and jumping out of bed, as he'd done all his working life. He went to the doctor, who gave him a little box. 'Try these,' said the doctor. 'What are they?' asked Smith, shaking the box. 'Sleeping pills?' 'No,' replied the doctor, 'drawing pins. Scatter some on the floor by your bed.'


'I've decided not to move to Florida when I retire. The climate disagrees with my wife. It's probably the bravest climate in the world.'

A retired couple consulted with an architect to build their dream home. The wife pointed to the plans. 'This window here means that the neighbours will be able to see me in the shower!' she said in horror.

'Don't worry dear,' said her husband. 'They'll only look once.'

What did Quasimodo get when he retired?

A lump sum and forty years' back pay.

'I'll certainly miss working. I love my work so much, I can sit and look at it for hours.'

'I'm retiring next week, my dear,' said a man to his wife, 'and I will be receiving a big lump sum. What would you like as a present? A diamond necklace, a car, a world cruise?'

'I want a divorce,' said his wife.

'I wasn't planning on spending that much,' replied the man.

'I see you've just turned sixty-four. When are you thinking of retiring?'

'Constantly.'


'I've decided to retire to Florida.'

'Florida? You'll hate it. It's a hundred degrees in the shade.'

'So? I don't have to stay in the shade, do I?'


'How are you finding your retirement?'

'Not too bad. I find I get the hardest part of the day over before breakfast.'

'What part's that?'

'Getting up.'

'My dad used to open for Yorkshire Cricket Club. When he finally retired, they installed automatic doors instead.'

I was involved in a hold up at the Post Office last week. Some old dear had lost her pension book.

*Reader's Digest* has filed for administration in the UK after failing to win pension scheme backing. Why didn't they just enter their own Prize Draw?

'Now that I've retired I've decided to spend my pension fund on essential surgery for me and my wife. Well, a boob job and a hair transplant don't come cheap...'

A husband and wife were discussing retirement. 'Here's our financial plan,' said the husband. 'We'll divorce at 65 and each marry someone else who planned better'.

Q. How do you get a million pound pension on retirement?

A. Invest ten million.


'I was a devoted board member until I retired.'

'Why did you retire?'

'I was de-voted!'


Ethel was retiring after 45 years' service in the same company. 'There isn't much in your collection, I'm afraid,' said her boss. 'Most of the people who liked you are dead.'


Bank managers don't retire, they just lose interest


Everyone needs a new hobby when they retire. After looking at my pension prediction I'm thinking of making mine 'hunting and gathering.'

'I'm not looking forward to my husband's retirement' said Doris to her neighbour. 'Less money, more him!'


'I hate to see you go,' said the boss, shaking Jones' hand firmly. 'I just don't know where we'll find someone who'll work for as little as you did.'


Employee: If don't start saving until I'm 40, at what age can I afford to retire comfortably?

Pensions adviser: 135.


Experts are advising that we should have a diversified pension plan. Mine is 30% hopes, 30% wishes and 40% prayers.


Retirement has finally given me the opportunity to turn over a new leaf. So I've bought a rake.


A man retired and told his wife he was going to spend his golden handshake on opening a French restaurant.

She agreed it would be an excellent idea. Three months later his wife phoned him and said 'Where on earth are you?' 'In France,' he replied.

Working life is like a roll of toilet paper. The nearer you get to the end, the faster it goes.

'You can afford to retire early,' said the pensions adviser to his client. 'I've worked out that on your last day you can go home at 4.30 instead of 5.00.'

'About your retirement, Gladys,' said the boss one morning. 'I've had an email from your husband saying he's willing to pay your salary if we'll keep you on.'

'Ah, retirement...' mused Jones one day. 'Endless freedom, sitting in a comfy chair in a lovely warm room drinking tea and surfing the net all day, in peace and quiet...do I really want to give all that up and stop coming into the office?'

When you retire you may find it helpful to organise household chores into categories, such as things you won't do now, things you won't do later, and things you'll never do.

Accountants don't retire, they just lose their balance

My husband and I used to work at our marriage. Now we're retired.

'The facts about your work here speak for themselves, Jones,' said the boss at the retirement party. 'My opinion, however, is in the letter with your P45.'

I got woken up by some idiot banging on my window the other day. There were at least five other counters open where he could have picked up his pension.

'Geoff always said he wanted to take up painting when he retired,' said Maureen to her friend. 'So I've got him painting the lounge, the bathroom, the kitchen, the bedroom….'

Before deciding to retire from your job, stay at home for a week and watch daytime television.

The key to a happy retirement is to have enough money to live on, but not enough to worry about.

One of the problems about retirement is that it gives you more time to read about the problems of retirement.

Grant me the senility to forget the people I never liked, the good fortune to run into the ones I do, and the eyesight to tell the difference.

I don't feel old. I don't feel anything until noon. Then it is time for my nap.

I retired early for health reasons – I was sick of work.

The biggest trouble with retiring is you end up having NOTHING to do and you can't tell when you are done.

Retirement is that point in life when you can't remember all the things you intended to do when you were still working.

Retired Royal Mail workers have been shocked to find out there will be a lot less money in their pension packets. If there's one thing a postman hates, it's opening an envelope and not finding any money inside.

You are ready for retirement when half the things in your shopping trolley say: 'For fast relief.'

**Retirement speech quips**

I'm not saying (name) is old, but when we cleared out his desk we found his ration book.

(Name) may be old, but he'll never be over the hill. Especially not in that car he drives.

There's no middle ground with (name). You either dislike him, or detest him.

We never knew (name) was an alcoholic, until he showed up one day sober.

(Name) is irreplaceable – which is why he never got promoted.

(Name of boss) never takes his work home with him. How can he? We do all the work.

We received a number of congratulatory emails for this event – from people congratulating themselves for not being here.

(Name) has always kept himself fit, by jumping to conclusions, pushing his luck and dodging work.

I'm not saying (name) is old, but he's the only man in this firm who still wears a demob suit.

I'd like to introduce a man who never says a bad word about anybody. He works in (department) so he doesn't know anybody.

We're here to say goodbye to (name) who has given this company ten years of loyal service, while being employed here for twenty years.

I'm not saying (name) has worked here too long, but his first computer was an Enigma machine.

(Name) started out in business with nothing, and he still has most of it.

Of all the secretaries you could have, (name) is the best type. Unfortunately, she's the worst typist.

(Name) has been here so long, he can remember when his company car was a bicycle.

(Name) was brought up to respect his elders. The trouble is, everyone he works with is younger than him.

I'm not saying (name) is in bad shape, but Accounts have started paying his wages weekly instead of monthly.

We've clubbed together to present (name) with a little item that's guaranteed to prevent car accidents. It's called a pensioner's bus pass.

(Name) decided to retire when he found out the candles on his birthday cake cost more than the cake itself.

(Name) still has plenty of life left in him. He's still chasing women, but only downhill.

(Name) still has his youthful good looks, although his side parting now covers most of his head.

Everyone in the company will miss (name). Just like everyone who's tried phoning him after 4pm on a Friday.

When (name) retires, he's planning to spend his time doing little jobs around the house. It's OK though, he's going to blame it on the dog.

### How people retire

Electricians are delighted.
Far Eastern diplomats are disoriented.
Jockeys are dismounted.
Piano tuners are unstrung.
Orchestra leaders are disbanded.
Artists' models are deposed.
Chiropodists are de-feeted.
Dressmakers are unbiased.
Office clerks are defiled.
Mediums are dispirited.
Programmers are decoded.
Pastry chefs are desserted.
Electricians are defused.

Underwear models are debriefed.
Painters are discoloured.
Judges are disappointed.
Mathematicians are discounted.
Tree surgeons disembark.


'I pick up my mother's pension for her every week.'

'That's very thoughtful of you.'

'Yes, and I always put flowers on her grave as well.'


Retirement is when your wife realizes she never gave your secretary enough sympathy.


'The vicar's retiring and the congregation's getting some money together to buy him a present. Would you like to contribute?'

'I don't think so. Every Sunday for years he's announced there will be a retiring collection. He must have enough by now!'

Brown was retiring from an accountancy firm and the boss asked him what he'd like for a gift. 'I will leave that up to you, sir,' said Brown, 'but if it is any help, I calculate that in the 35 years I have worked here, I have contributed to 23 retirement collections, 14 maternity collections, 8 redundancy collections and two bereavement collections. Adjusted for inflation and the cost of living index, the present ought to be worth something in the region of £273.76.'

A few days later it was the retirement party and the boss handed Brown an envelope. 'I thought over what you said, Brown, and I calculated that in the 35 years you have worked here, you have consumed 4673 teabags, 15 pounds of sugar, 18 gallons of milk, 250 rolls of toilet paper, three chairs, and worn out two square yards of carpet. Please accept this cheque for 29 pence.'

You know it's time to retire when you know all the answers, but nobody asks you any questions.

Smith in Marketing thought it was time to move on to greener pastures. The trouble was, he was too old to climb the fence.

The longer your career, the better you realise you were.

'I sometimes look through that window next to your office door,' mused Perkins to his boss, 'and catch sight of an old boy in the building next door, white haired, hunched over his desk, peering short-sightedly at his work. I always say to myself I'll retire when I look like that.' 'In that case, you'd better clear your desk,' said the boss. 'That's not a window, it's a mirror!'

'When I retire, I'm going to move to Bulgaria with my wife.'

'Sofia?'

'No, Maureen.'

'My pensions advisor told me to make a sound investment, so I blew my lump sum on an expensive stereo.'

Pensions advisor (to client): According to my calculations...you should have died last year.

# More joke books from Montpelier Publishing

Available from Amazon

The Book of Church Jokes

After Dinner Laughs (Volumes 1 and 2)

Jewish Jokes

Medical Jokes

Scottish Jokes

Welsh Jokes

Large Print Jokes

Large Print Wordsearch

The Bumper Book of Riddles, Puzzles and Rhymes

Wedding Jokes

A Little Book of Limericks

Take My Wife: Hilarious Jokes of Love and Marriage

The Old Fashioned Joke Book (Volumes 1 and 2)

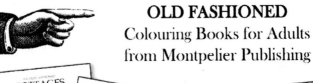